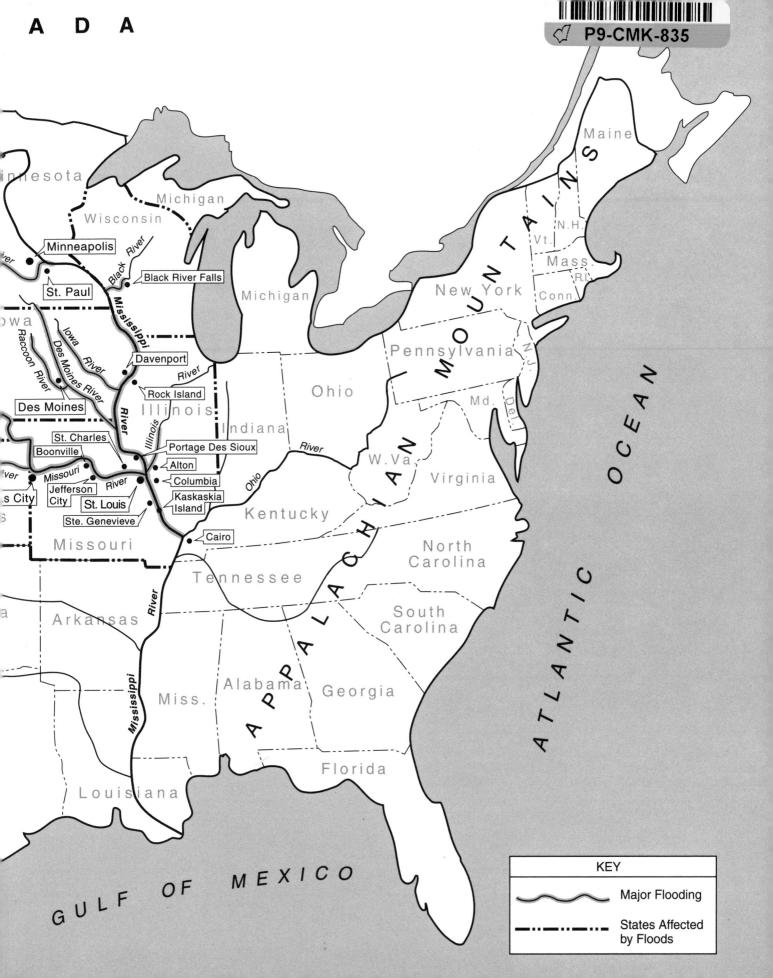

The Great Midwest Flood

by Carole Garbuny Vogel

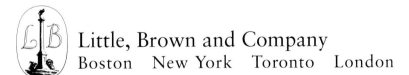

Little, Brown and Company
Boston   New York   Toronto   London

To my mother-in-law, Lydia C. Vogel
and in memory of my father-in-law, Arthur Vogel

Acknowledgments

I would like to thank the following people for their technical assistance: Claude N. Strauser, Chief of Potamology Section, Hydrologic and Hydraulics Branch, U.S. Army Corps of Engineers, St. Louis District, for his expertise and his ability to communicate complex ideas in layman's terms; Bill Redding, Sierra Club's Mississippi River Basin Ecoregion Program Director in the Midwest Office, for his insight and criticism; Susie Stonner, Public Information Officer for the State of Missouri Emergency Management Agency, for her critique; and Coralee Paull for her capable assistance with research. I would also like to acknowledge the help of the dozens of other people who took time from their busy schedules to answer my questions. Where the opinions of experts conflicted, I used my own judgment in presenting the information.

I am indebted to my husband, Mark A. Vogel, for telling me what worked and what didn't. A special thanks to fellow writers Susan Sekuler, Barbara Ehrlich White, and especially Florence Harris, for writing advice. I am particularly grateful to my astute agent, Reneé Cho of McIntosh and Otis, Inc., and my wonderful editor, Hilary Breed, for making the work of writing fun.

First Edition

Photography credits: © AP/Wide World Photos, by Eric Draper, p. 21 left; © AP/Wide World Photos, by James A. Finley, p. 3; © AP/Wide World Photos, by E. J. Flynn, p. 31 right; © AP/Wide World Photos, by Tannen Maury, p. 11 bottom; © AP/Wide World Photos, by Stephan Savoia, p. 11 top; photograph by Nick Decker, Missouri Department of Natural Resources, pp. 15 bottom, 22, 31 left; © Susan Warren Deixler, pp. 4, 8 bottom, 15 top; photograph © *The Des Moines Register,* by Harry Baumert, pp. 13, 17, 25 bottom; photograph © *The Des Moines Register,* by Paul Hiscocks, p. 19; photographs © *The Des Moines Register,* by Bob Modersohn, p. 28; © EOSAT, p. 8 top; © Peter Hawkins, p. 5 top; Illinois Department of Transportation, p. 7; © Larry Mayer, pp. 12, 18; © News Tribune, by Julie Smith, p. 29 top; © News Tribune, by Shaun T. Zimmerman, pp. 25 top, 29 bottom; © Frank Oberle, pp. 14, 16 bottom, 23 bottom, 27; © *The Quad-City Times,* pp. 1, 9, 10, 30; © Charlie Rahm, U.S. Department of Agriculture, p. 32; © Ted Reisinger, pp. 16 top, 20 top and bottom, 21 right; U.S. Army Corps of Engineers, New Orleans District, pp. 5 bottom, 6; U.S. Army Corps of Engineers, St. Louis District, pp. 23 top, 26 top and bottom; The White House, p. 19 top; Mike Wright, Missouri Highway and Transportation Department, p. 24 top and bottom.

Library of Congress Cataloging-in-Publication Data

Vogel, Carole Garbuny.
  The great Midwest flood / Carole Garbuny Vogel.—1st ed.
    p. cm.
  ISBN 0-316-90248-9
  1. Floods—Middle West—History—20th century—Juvenile literature. 2. Floods—Middle West—Pictorial works—Juvenile literature. 3. Middle West—History—Juvenile literature. 4. Middle West—Pictorial works—Juvenile Literature. I. Title.
  F355.V64 1995
  363.3'493'097709049—dc20   94-45778

10 9 8 7 6 5 4 3 2 1
SC
Published simultaneously in Canada
by Little, Brown & Company (Canada) Limited

Printed in Hong Kong

AN EARTHQUAKE DOES ITS DAMAGE in seconds. Tornadoes wreak havoc in minutes. But the great flood of 1993 was a slow-motion disaster. It crept into the valleys of the Midwest, fanned out, and lingered for months.

In 1993, spring and summer storms drenched the upper Midwest, filling rivers and soaking the ground. The rain kept falling, and by June, the Mississippi and other rivers had risen to dangerous levels. Raging waters burst through levees and roared across the land. Soon the river valleys of the Midwest turned into a vast inland sea. The flood claimed at least 38 lives, damaged 100,000 homes, and caused about 17 billion dollars worth of destruction.

Rushing water from a levee break in Columbia, Illinois, demolished these buildings shortly after the photograph was taken.

Almost every river and stream between the Allegheny Mountains and the Rockies leads to the Mississippi. This tremendous river begins as a shallow creek that springs from Minnesota's small Lake Itaska. On its 2,350-mile journey to the Gulf of Mexico, it collects water from 31 states and two Canadian provinces. Many of its 100,000 tributaries are mere streams, while others, such as the Missouri and Ohio Rivers, are formidable rivers in their own right.

The Mississippi and its tributaries played a major role in the growth of the nation. Pioneers boated into the interior of the continent and built their farms and villages near riverbanks to remain close to water and shipping routes. To divert floods, the settlers erected dirt mounds. Over time, these mounds were turned into levees: large earthen walls that stretched for miles and miles along the rivers. However, these levees were not strong enough to hold back deluges.

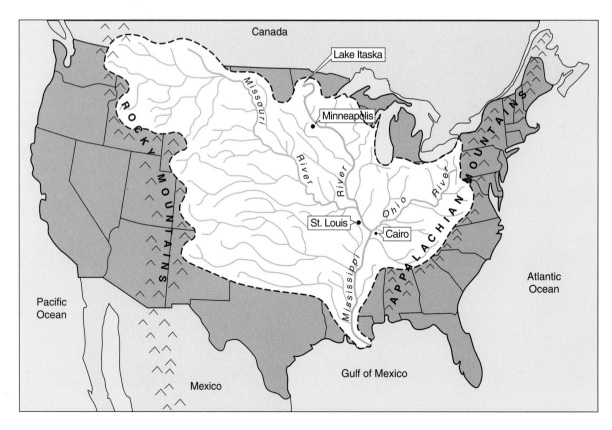

Heavy rainfall in one part of the Mississippi River Basin can send raging floodwaters careening downriver to other areas.

After a disastrous flood in the spring of 1927, the U.S. Congress voted to tame the Mississippi and its tributaries. Since then, billions of dollars have been spent on flood management and the maintenance of shipping lanes. Much of the river's channel was scooped out to make it deeper for barges and boats. Nearly 100 major reservoirs were constructed throughout the entire Upper Mississippi Basin. In 1993, many of these reservoirs filled to capacity, flooding land that had been set aside upstream to prevent even worse flooding downstream.

Millions of Americans live near the banks of the immense Mississippi River system and rely on it for drinking water and sanitation. The rivers and streams irrigate and fertilize some of the richest farmland in the nation. About 6,388 miles of the Mississippi and its branches can handle shipping traffic. Competing with humans for space in and along the waterways are beavers, muskrats, otters, and other wildlife.

The mighty Mississippi River at its source: Lake Itaska, in Minnesota.

The Mississippi forms the backbone of a vast aquatic highway system. A fleet of 20,000 barges shuttles back and forth along the river, hauling grain, coal, petroleum, and other cargo.

Floods are nature's way of cleaning riverbeds. Normally rivers lack the energy to move the mud, sand, and other debris that collects on the bottom. Quickly moving floodwaters flush out these materials and carry them onto the floodplain—the flat land on either side of the banks. When the floodwaters slowly roll away from the floodplain, they leave a layer of silt that enriches the soil.

Before levees were constructed, the Mississippi meandered across a wide floodplain and changed course frequently. Marshes, backwaters, and other wetlands bordered the river channel. Their waterlogged soils were too wet to support crops, but their plants provided nourishment for water birds and other animals. Occasionally mammoth floods rampaged through the floodplain, uprooting trees, stripping away soil, and carving up the riverbanks.

Levees changed the floodplain landscape by pinning the river to a channel less than a mile wide. Behind these massive structures, farmers drained the wetlands and turned them into farmland. Levee construction also flourished along the Missouri and other midwestern rivers. Throughout the region, much of the wetlands disappeared, as did the fish and wildlife they supported.

Locks and dams on the Mississippi maintain sufficient water depth for navigation and recreation during periods of low and normal flow. These dams, however, do not play a role in flood control.

During the flood of 1993, more than 1,000 of the nonfederal levees gave way. However, only 40 of the levees built by the U.S. Army Corps of Engineers were overpowered.

The placement of levees in the Upper Mississippi Basin was not coordinated by any central authority. The U.S. Army Corps of Engineers built only 226 of the approximately 1,600 levees erected. Many owners of riverfront land put up their own structures or banded together into levee districts to build and maintain levees. These structures usually lacked the strength of federal levees.

Attracted by fertile soil and cheap property, people moved onto the land taken from the rivers. New and higher levees gave floodplain dwellers a false sense of security and encouraged the development of high-risk areas.

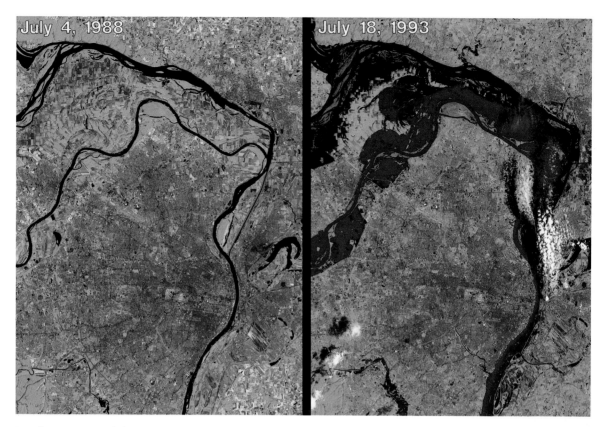

July 4, 1988   July 18, 1993

Satellite images of the St. Louis area reveal the dramatic differences between water levels in a drought year, 1988, and those reached near the flood's peak in 1993.

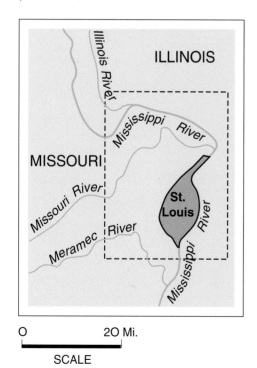

Illinois River

ILLINOIS

Mississippi River

MISSOURI

Missouri River

Missouri River

Meramec River

St. Louis

Mississippi River

Mississippi River

O   20 Mi.

SCALE

The wet autumn of 1992, compounded by substantial snowmelt the next spring, filled rivers and soaked the ground in the upper Midwest. When heavy summer rains fell, the bloated soil could not soak them up. The land was like a bucket full to the brim; the rainwater spilled across it into already swollen streams and rivers. When the streams and rivers soon filled to capacity, they poured water back onto the land.

Throughout the summer of 1993, rain drenched the Mississippi River Basin. It seemed as though Mother Nature had forgotten to turn off the faucet. Why? Blame it on the jet stream, the river of air that flows high above the earth. In a normal summer, the jet stream snakes across Canada. But in 1993, it dipped into the Midwest, pulling down cold, dry air from the north. At the same time, warm moist air streamed up from the Gulf of Mexico. When the warm air and cold air collided, they triggered thunderstorms and drenching rains.

Usually when a mass of warm air and a mass of cold air meet, one overpowers the other and forces it out. That summer, however, the air masses were evenly matched. Neither could move the other, and the storm system stalled over the Midwest. The rains kept coming. And coming. And coming.

Like a recurring nightmare, almost daily cloudbursts upriver sent even more water to flood-weary communities downstream.

Ordinarily rainfall is measured in inches. In 1993, it was measured in feet. The soggiest areas—portions of Kansas and Missouri—received three-and-a-half feet or more between April and August.

In the beginning, the rising rivers splashed over the farmlands on their banks. Long accustomed to flooding, the farmers waited for the water to subside. But as the weeks dragged by, the rivers barely budged. Instead, by the end of planting season, the water began to creep higher and higher, lapping against silos, barns, and homes. Inch by inch, the rivers claimed land thought to be far from their reach.

Normally the upper Midwest produces most of the nation's corn and soybeans, but not in 1993. Even in areas untouched by floods, the rains turned many fields into lakes or left the soil too soggy to plant. Where crops could be planted, heavy rains and little sunshine stunted their growth. Plant diseases thrived in the humid weather, reducing crops even further.

By the time flooding was over, 8 million acres of farmland had been swamped and another 12 million were too waterlogged to grow anything at all.

These goats and cows were fortunate: Rushing water from levee breaks sometimes swept away pigs, chickens, and other farm animals in its path.

On Father's Day, June 20, floodgates malfunctioned at a hydroelectric dam in Hatfield, Wisconsin. The dam overflowed, and the water cascaded down the Black River. In the town of Black River Falls, floodwaters overtopped a levee and swallowed a low-lying neighborhood up to the rooftops.

To protect threatened neighborhoods, residents constructed new levees using sandbags.

Meanwhile, in Minnesota, the Mississippi was peaking in the Twin Cities of Minneapolis and St. Paul. On June 26, the high water rose about five feet above the normal riverbank but caused little damage. However, rivers and streams throughout the upper Midwest continued to expand with the pummeling storms.

Midwesterners were worried. How big would this flood get? Before levees were built, colossal floods had been contained by bluffs, steep cliffs that overlook rivers. The distance between opposing bluffs on either side of the Mississippi Valley averaged three to six miles from Davenport, Iowa, to the Ohio River, a 493-mile stretch. Residents feared that the river would overpower the levees and fill this vast valley bluff to bluff once again.

Following a levee break in early July, the Iowa River wrenched this two-story house from its foundation. Fortunately nobody was inside at the time.

In a frantic effort to hold back the water, residents reinforced levees with sandbags. The majority of these levees were designed to defend against a "50-year flood," a deluge with a 2 percent chance of happening in any given year. In most places the flood of 1993 loomed much bigger, swelling into a 125-year event—an immense flood with less than a 1 percent chance of occurring in any given year.

It would have been a miracle if the levees had staved off the floodwaters. Unlike dams, they are not designed to hold back water continuously. The bloated rivers washed over, seeped through, tunneled under, scoured away, or punched holes in nearly 70 percent of the levees in the flood zone. When a breach, or gap, formed, floodwaters blew through with the roar of a freight train and fanned out over the land.

Giant whirlpools form when a river tunnels beneath a levee and begins to drain behind it.

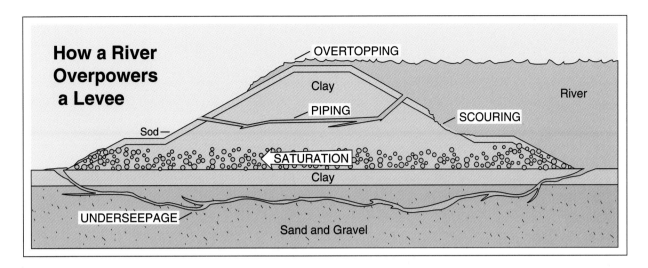

How a River Overpowers a Levee

OVERTOPPING

Clay

PIPING

SCOURING

River

Sod

SATURATION

Clay

UNDERSEEPAGE

Sand and Gravel

Overtopping: The river flows over the top of a levee like a waterfall and quickly washes away the land side.

Piping: The river tunnels through animal burrows or through holes formed by plant roots. Then it widens its path and erodes the levee from the inside.

Saturation: The river gradually seeps into the levee and weakens it until the structure crumbles.

Scouring: The current scours dirt away from the base of the levee.

Underseepage: The ground becomes saturated and allows water to seep beneath the levee. The water bubbles up on the dry side and turns the surrounding ground into quicksand. If the bubbling water is muddy, it is a sign that the river is undermining the levee. The levee is in immediate danger of collapse. On the other hand, if clear water gurgles up, it means the water is being filtered by the ground and is not in direct contact with the river. The seepage can be controlled by ringing the bubbling water with sandbags and filling the enclosure with water to equalize the water pressure.

The Missouri River defeated this levee near Boonville, Missouri.

The battle against the rising rivers played out slowly over weeks and months. Just when the water would start to recede, more rain would send it to higher levels. The levees, designed to retain high water for days, not weeks, began to give way like sand castles overpowered by an encroaching tide.

Neighbors pitched in to help neighbors. And strangers gathered to protect the homes and businesses of people they had never met (*top*). Members of the National Guard formed a human chain to pass sandbags along a levee (*bottom*).

Jill Masonholder, age 11, hefted sandbags at Columbus Junction, Iowa. Each bag weighed about 35 pounds.

As the water rolled across the Midwest, donations of time, money, and relief goods flooded in from near and far. Volunteers housed the homeless and distributed food and clothing. The American Red Cross, the Salvation Army, and various government agencies organized a human brigade to battle the rivers and help flood victims. City dwellers and college students worked side by side with hog farmers and senior citizens.

Many of the thousands of volunteers worked in pairs to fill sandbags. One person held the bag open. The other shoveled in sand, leaving some space so the bag would lie flat when put in place. After the bags were tied, other volunteers hoisted them onto the levees. To keep the new barriers dry, workers wrapped them in plastic sheeting.

On the night of July 8, a monster thunderstorm boomed over central Iowa, illuminating the sky and dumping as much as 10 inches of rain. The water quickly ran off the soggy soil into the Raccoon River, turning the already swollen river into a great, angry torrent that raced downstream toward Des Moines.

On July 11, the river tumbled over the 15-foot levee protecting Des Moines' water treatment plant and forced the facility to shut down. For 12 days, a quarter million people endured life without tap water for drinking, bathing, or flushing toilets.

Drinking water was trucked to distribution sites throughout the area. Clutching milk jugs, juice bottles, and other containers, people lined up to collect a gallon or two at a time. To flush toilets, residents captured rainwater, drained hot water heaters, and even emptied swimming pools and water beds. Even after running water was restored, it was not safe to drink for an additional seven days.

John O'Donnell Stadium, home to Davenport's minor league baseball team, became a symbol of the flood's tyranny.

Sandbag walls failed to protect Davenport, Iowa, the largest city on the Mississippi without a protective levee. On July 4, a concerned President Bill Clinton came to survey the damage.

State workers await their turn to use portable toilets in Des Moines after the city lost its water supply.

Although some people showered in the rain, most cut down on their bathing, which soon became obvious.

Throughout the Midwest, other cities and towns suffered the same fate. Altogether, floodwaters contaminated the water treatment plants of 200 municipalities.

Uniformed National Guard troops became commonplace as they assisted in the struggle against the flood.

Members of the National Guard and the U.S. Coast Guard helped residents flee flooded neighborhoods.

Four miles above St. Louis, the Missouri, one of the longest rivers in North America, joins the mighty Mississippi in a wild, swirling current. St. Charles County, Missouri, is sandwiched on the peninsula between the two giant waterways—a treacherous location in 1993. Despite heroic efforts by sandbaggers, levee after levee gave way. On July 16, the Missouri River merged with the Mississippi 20 miles upstream from its usual meeting point.

At the flood's peak, almost half of St. Charles County was submerged in cocoa-colored water as deep as 20 feet. Ten thousand people fled their homes. Like other flood victims throughout the Midwest, many crowded into the houses of friends or relatives, checked into motels, or camped in cars, tents, and recreational vehicles. Some found refuge in shelters run by the Red Cross or the Salvation Army. Swollen rivers left people homeless for days, weeks, or months. Many people had no homes left to return to.

On July 30, the Missouri inflicted its most devastating blow in St. Charles County. The levee protecting Chesterfield Valley, a high-tech industrialized area, gave way just hours after officials had evacuated residents and workers. Water engulfed 500 businesses, an airport, a jail, and a sewage treatment plant. Raw sewage from 75,000 homes spilled into the river.

Throughout the flood zone, floodwaters swamped a total of 388 waste-water treatment plants. The sewage-laced river water reeked, and it carried the potential for illnesses ranging from diarrhea and hepatitis to diphtheria and tetanus.

Determined midwesterners found ways to get on with their lives (*above*).

Despite waist-deep water, many people chose to remain in flood-stricken areas. The owner of this market in Portage Des Sioux, Missouri, permitted town residents to take what they needed free of charge (*left*).

TV crews and newspaper reporters flocked to the Midwest to cover the unfolding flood drama. The battle to save Ste. Genevieve, Missouri, the nation's oldest town west of the Mississippi, made a particularly compelling story. The town, with its vertical log houses built in the late 1700s and early 1800s, appeared doomed. In a heroic effort, residents, volunteers, and National Guard troops barricaded Ste. Genevieve with sand, gravel, and a half million sandbags.

The makeshift flood wall stretched for more than three miles and rose as high as 20 feet. Emergency workers patrolled the levee day and night for signs of collapse. Despite serious inroads by the river, the people of Ste. Genevieve succeeded in saving much of their heritage, giving the watching world at least one happy ending.

"The Great Wall of Ste. Genevieve," a makeshift levee, survived the worst of the flooding, thanks to the effort of hundreds of volunteers.

Most towns weren't as lucky. Across the river from Ste. Genevieve, the Mississippi suddenly tunneled beneath the levee protecting Kaskaskia Island. As the barrier gave way, the river tore a 350-foot hole through it. Floodwaters whipped across Kaskaskia, covering the 15,000-acre island within hours.

In places such as Alton, Illinois, the levees held, but the Mississippi outflanked them by backing up through sewers and flooding the city from within. All through the flood zone, rivers backed into sewer pipes and gushed into homes through toilets and drains. More than half the flood-ravaged homes were damaged this way.

The Kaskaskia Island Levee was tall enough to prevent over-topping, but piping caused this breach.

Within hours of the breach, water covered Kaskaskia Island.

When the river valleys of the Midwest filled with water, a transportation crisis erupted. High water idled river traffic, anchoring thousands of barges from the end of June until late August or September.

Creeks and streams everywhere topped their banks, washing out roads and sloshing over bridges. Detours of 100 miles were not unusual. At one point, all the bridges along a 300-mile stretch of the Mississippi, from Davenport to St. Louis, were closed. Traffic backed up for hours on the few usable roadways.

Floodwaters covered this highway near Jefferson City, Missouri (*above*). When the water receded, only broken pavement remained (*below*).

Railroad tracks along the rivers disappeared beneath the rushing current, forcing railroads to reroute 30 percent of the nation's rail freight.

As the rivers clawed through the floodplain, they snapped utility poles and ruptured gas lines. Communities were left without electricity, telephones, or gas for cooking. Not even the dead remained safe from the river's grip. In Hardin, Missouri, the rampaging Missouri River unearthed more than 750 graves from a 180-year-old cemetery. Bones spilled into the turgid river, and floodwaters washed some coffins nearly 20 miles downstream.

Canoes and boats became the only reliable means of transportation on flooded streets. Submerged cars, stop signs, and mailboxes created "road" hazards.

St. Louis before the flood. St. Louis is the largest midwestern city on the Mississippi. In a typical summer, the average depth of the Mississippi is about 23 feet when it flows past the arch.

Flood control reservoirs in the upper Midwest reduced by three feet the flooding that hit St. Louis. As a result, this 54-foot-high, 11-mile-long barrier was sufficient to protect the business district and low-lying neighborhoods of St. Louis.

Unrelenting rainfall propelled the rivers of the Midwest to some of the highest levels ever recorded. Concrete flood walls protected Kansas City, Rock Island, in Illinois, and most other urban areas. The 54-foot flood wall in St. Louis held back the Mississippi when it crested at a record-setting 49.6 feet on August 1. Nevertheless, St. Louis faced some scary moments.

At the flood's peak, the Mississippi carried 7.8 million gallons of water per second past the arch. This is 11 times the average flow rate over Niagara Falls and is equal to more than a million fire hydrants flowing wide open.

The powerful current dislodged the Spirit of the River entertainment complex. The complex, consisting of a cluster of boats normally moored near the Gateway Arch, swirled downstream at a fast clip. Its floating Burger King restaurant and World War II minesweeper slammed into the city's largest bridge and continued onward. Tugboats corralled the breakaway vessels before they could collide with the flood wall.

Fifty miles south of St. Louis, the flood finally lost its wallop. At Cairo, Illinois, the Mississippi joined the Ohio River and moved into a bigger channel. There the floodwater was accommodated by the larger riverbed in the same way a traffic jam disperses when a clogged two-lane road turns into a superhighway.

In August, the rains tapered off at last and the rivers began to give back the land. As the water slowly retreated, the flood zone took on the appearance of a junkyard. Broken glass, twisted metal, splintered boards, and other debris littered the landscape. Lakes of sewage water lingered on fields, and a slick, foul-smelling scum coated streets and buildings. A nauseating stench hung over entire neighborhoods.

Many homes and businesses had simply vanished. Others were damaged beyond repair. For the remainder, the mopping, sopping, scraping, and scrubbing began. The demand for disinfectants, rubber gloves, scrub brushes, shovels, and other cleaning tools replaced the need for sandbags. Pumping out water was the easy part. Dealing with warped floors, rotted walls, mildewed furniture, and mud-caked plumbing fixtures was much more diffi-

cult. The oozing muck had ruined everything it touched—carpets, chairs, sofas, beds, refrigerators, microwave ovens, TVs, CD players, VCRs, toys, photographs, and keepsakes. For many people, the worst part was coping with the snakes, worms, frogs, toads, and other creatures that had taken up residence in their homes. In some communities the cleanup proved to be premature as fall rains brought new floods.

The New American Gothic

Floodwaters slosh against the stained glass windows of the Methodist church in north Jefferson City, Missouri (*above*). Receding floodwaters left an eight-inch layer of muck on the church floor. Stains on the wall mark the river's reach (*below*).

Larry Miller, an employee of the Davenport Recreation Department, tackles the cleanup of John O'Donnell Stadium.

In the aftermath of the flood, midwesterners confronted the muddy issues it had raised. Many people blamed levees for the unprecedented flood heights. Constricted river channels did force water to flow higher, but along the Mississippi and Missouri Rivers, massive flood control reservoirs generally counteracted this rise in flood levels. The reservoirs held back water upstream, lowering flood heights downstream. Many of these reservoirs filled completely and could not hold more water. Massive amounts of rain fell downstream from the reservoirs and could not be captured. There was simply too much water and no place to put it.

Flood waves created by the overtopping and breaching of levees along the swiftly moving Missouri produced tremendous erosion. Rushing water scoured out holes 25 to 50 feet deep and deposited thick layers of sand behind broken levees.

On a natural floodplain, meandering river channels provide a buffer against small floods. Their large, snaking curves fill up and serve as temporary reservoirs, slowing and weakening floodwaters. Rising water spreads out more slowly and causes less erosion. Wetland soil soaks up excess water and plants impede the flow. However, if the natural vegetation is removed because of development behind the riverbank, water quickly runs off the soaked land. Thus, development throughout the Mississippi River valley added to flood heights.

Restoring some of the lost wetlands will give rivers more room to spread out during moderate to large floods but will have no impact on major ones. The main benefit of wetlands restoration is not flood control but the increase of available habitats for plants, fish, and wildlife.

Thick sand deposits resulting from levee breaks turned productive farmland into useless fields.

After learning that all her toys were ruined, Heidi Ackleson, age 4, is comforted by her mother at their flood-ravaged home in Des Moines, Iowa.

31

The real disaster that occurred in 1993 was not that the flood took place, but that people and buildings were in the way. The Midwest needs a plan that balances human uses of floodplains with the forces of nature. Decisions made about floodplain management now can determine whether future floods will or will not be disasters.

Policy makers suggested several ways to reduce potential destruction. The government can purchase property in flood-prone areas and help residents relocate to safer places. Official agencies can discourage flood victims from returning to hazardous areas by changing insurance programs and disaster relief efforts that encourage rebuilding. Farmers can implement agricultural methods that reduce runoff and keep more water and soil on cropland. Agricultural levees can be designed to permit controlled flooding when rivers rise too high. These measures will not prevent or reduce epic floods. They will, however, reduce the harmful impact of floods on people and their communities.

The streams and rivers of the upper Midwest will swell again. Most floods will be relatively small. But someday another massive deluge will roar through the land, and the rivers will once more reclaim their floodplains.

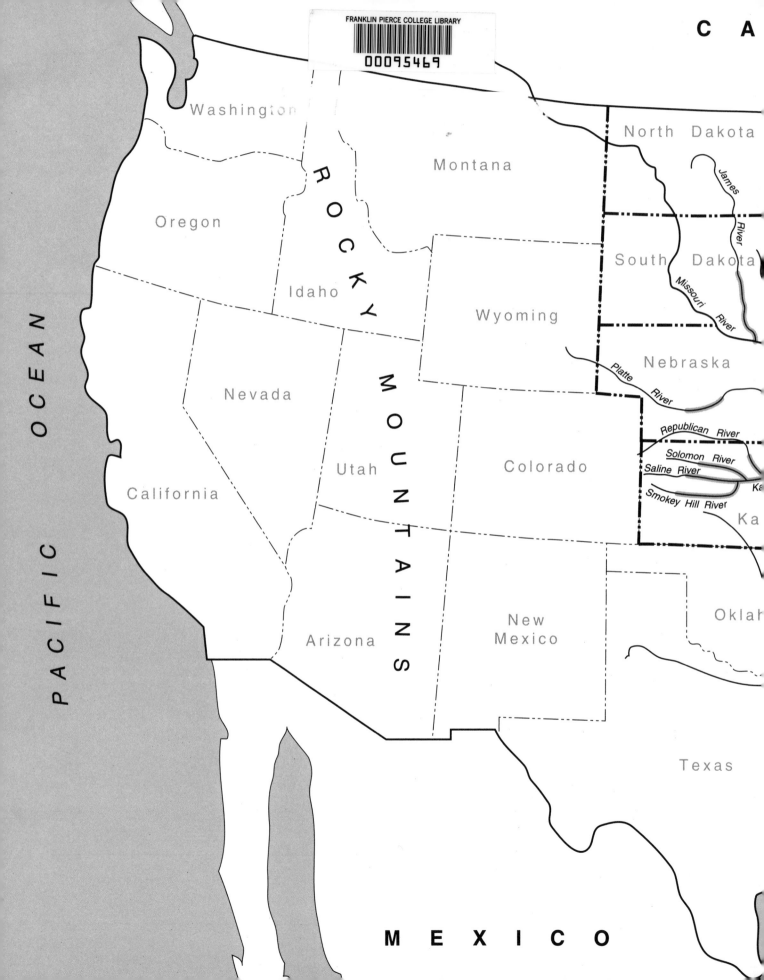